ADVENTURE (

The H
Railwa

based on Enid Blyton's
Five go off to Camp

Illustrated by Gary Rees

HODDER AND STOUGHTON
LONDON SYDNEY AUCKLAND TORONTO

British Library Cataloguing in Publication Data
Famous Five adventure games.

The haunted railway game.
1. Games—Juvenile literature
2. Adventure and adventurers—Juvenile literature
I. Blyton, Enid
793'.9 GV1203.

ISBN 0-340-35870-X

First published 1984

Published by Hodder and Stoughton Children's Books,
a division of Hodder and Stoughton Ltd, Mill Road,
Dunton Green, Sevenoaks, Kent TN13 2YJ

Printed in Hong Kong

You have often read about The Famous Five's adventures . . . Now here's your chance to take part in one!

This time YOU are in charge. YOU have to work out the clues, read the maps, crack the codes. Whether The Five solve the mystery or not is in your hands.

You will not necessarily solve the mystery on your first attempt. It may well take several goes. Keep trying, though, and you will eventually be successful.

Even when you *have* solved the mystery, the game can still be played again. For there are many different routes to the solution – and each route involves different clues and adventures.

So the game can be played over and over . . . as many times as you like!

HOW TO PLAY

To solve the mystery, you have to go with The Five on an adventure through the book. You do this by starting at PARAGRAPH ONE and then following the instructions to other paragraphs.

Many of the paragraphs will ask you to work out some sort of clue. You do not have to work out every one of the clues to solve the final mystery . . . but the more you manage, the more you're likely to be successful. The less clues you crack, the less chance of completing the adventure.

To help you work out the clues, there are several pieces of equipment available – a compass, a map, a pair of binoculars and a code-book. You can start with only *one* of these EQUIPMENT CARDS but you will often pick up others as the game goes along. Occasionally, however, you will be asked to give them up as well.

To hold your EQUIPMENT CARDS during the adventure, there is a RUCKSACK CARD. This will tell you exactly which EQUIPMENT CARDS you have for assistance at any one time. Any EQUIPMENT CARDS not in your rucksack **are not to be used or consulted** – and therefore should be kept out of play.

Of course, no Famous Five adventure could take place without provisions. You are therefore given three PICNIC CARDS. These are to be kept in the slit of the LUNCHBOX CARD.

Every time The Five eat or lose some of their provisions during the adventure, you must remove one of the PICNIC CARDS from your LUNCHBOX. When there are no PICNIC CARDS left in your LUNCHBOX, the provisions have run out and so you cannot possibly continue with the adventure. The game is over and you will have to start again from the beginning.

READY TO START

The Famous Five are JULIAN (the biggest and eldest), DICK, GEORGE (real name Georgina, but she always wanted to be a boy), ANNE and George's dog, TIMMY.

They have gone for a camping holiday on the bleak, lonely moors. The nearest village is a good five miles away and the only place for food is a little farm at the bottom of their hill. On the farm lives a boy, Jock, and they soon make friends with him. They also like his mother but they are rather less keen on his stepfather, who runs the farm. His name is Mr. Andrews and he seems a very moody sort of person.

On one of The Five's visits to the farm, Jock tells them a strange tale. From his bedroom window he can just about see an old stretch of railway line which runs along the moors. It was supposed to have been abandoned a long time ago but on some nights he has noticed a strange yellow glow from that direction. He is convinced that it is an old steam train still shunting back and forth!

The Five become very intrigued by this story and ask Jock where the old line is so they can go and investigate. Just as Jock is about to tell them, however, his stepfather walks in and insists on knowing what they are talking about. When he finds out, he goes into a rage. He says that the train is a ghost train, operated by evil forces, and they had better stay well clear of it.

The Five pretend to take heed of his warning but secretly have other ideas in mind! As soon as they return to their tents, they prepare to go in search of this mysterious train . . .

To join them on this search, you will first of all need to put on your rucksack. So pick out the RUCKSACK CARD and have it near to you. You must now choose a piece of equipment to take with you. The Five each have a compass, a map, a pair of binoculars and a codebook - but you can start with only *one* of these. Which do you think would be the most useful? Insert the EQUIPMENT CARD you have chosen into the slit of your RUCKSACK CARD and keep the remaining three EQUIPMENT CARDS out of play until told you can pick them up.

Now for the provisions. Jock's mother has kindly prepared a delicious picnic of sandwiches, cherry cake and ginger beer. Put the three PICNIC CARDS into the slit of your LUNCHBOX CARD. Don't forget to remove a PICNIC CARD every time The Five eat or lose some of their provisions.

Remember: When there are no PICNIC CARDS left in your LUNCHBOX, the adventure has to stop and you must start all over again.

Good luck!

The
in the
Cupboard
Joke book
GW00793119

Illustrated by David Farris

Hippo Books
Scholastic Publications Limited
London

Scholastic Publications Ltd.,
10 Earlham Street, London WC2H 9RX, UK

Scholastic Publications Ltd.,
10 Earlham Street, London WC2H 9RX, UK

Scholastic Inc.,
730 Broadway, New York, NY 10003, USA

Scholastic Tab Publications Ltd.,
123 Newkirk Road, Richmond Hill,
Ontario L4C 3G5, Canada

Ashton Scholastic Pty. Ltd.,
P O Box 579, Gosford, New South Wales,
Australia

Ashton Scholastic Ltd.,
165 Marua Road, Panmure, Auckland 6,
New Zealand

First published 1989

ISBN 0 590 76125 0

Made and printed by Cox and Wyman Ltd.,
Reading, Berks.

Typeset in Plantin by COLLAGE (Design in Print),
Longfield Hill, Kent.

CONTENTS

Introduction

Hi!

We thought it would be a good idea to put together this *Skeleton in the Cupboard* joke book because — no fooling — we live with our dad in cemetery lodge, as the photo below shows. You may think it's pretty weird living in a cemetery, but we like it. And it's very popular. People are dying to get into our cemetery!

Besides, we've got some very nice neighbours: there's *Count Dracula*, who lives in a big, creepy house overlooking the cemetery with Lady Dracula and their son, the Honourable Drogo, and daughter, Creepella.

We have lots of friends living in the cemetery, too. *Gilda the Ghost* haunts a big crypt in the middle and gives such good Halloween parties that she's known as "The Ghostess With the Mostest". Her son *Grimly* comes home regularly from University (he goes to Boo U.!) and always brings some fiends — sorry, friends — with him. And *Wanda the Witch* lives in a little semi-detached mausoleum near the cemetery wall with her black cat *Rasputin*. She's a lot nicer than she looks even if she can't stand her arch-rival, the *Red Witch*.

Then there's *Dr Frankenstein*, who's always prowling through the cemetery looking for spare parts. We always know that he's around when we hear him calling: "Yoo hoo! Is any body home?" You can bet that when Dr F is around, *Sam the Skeleton* and his friends keep hidden over in their corner of the cemetery near the big willow tree.

Another cemetery regular is *Gus, the Council Gravedigger*, who comes to work carrying his spade and lunch bucket every day. Gus loves work. He could just sit and watch it for hours. Not to mention *Mr Jolly*, the undertaker, who is a regular visitor and who once asked a little old lady attending one of his funerals: "Hardly worth all the trouble going home again, is it, dear?"

One thing we enjoy about living in a cemetery is all of the interesting tombstones. It's almost like a library except you can't take any of them home. The one we like best is inscribed: "Not Sleeping, Just Dead". We enjoy our cemetery best on Halloween when *Gilda* gives a big party and invites all the neighbours to meet her friends — famous ghosts, spirits, phantoms and spectres from every age and all around the world. She even invites *Sam the Skeleton*, though she has to lock up her spirit dog, *Ghostly*, when *Sam* is around.

If you're ever in our neighbourhood, we hope you'll drop by in the cemetery and visit us. You'll really dig it! In the meantime, we hope you will enjoy our collection of spooktacular jokes in a jugular vein.

Love

Josh & Jake

Halloween Howlers

Count Dracula's pet, Batula, came racing in through the window and skidded to a halt on the desktop. "Quick, master!" the bat said. "Is my bite poisonous or what?"

"Of course it is," said Dracula. "What of it?"

"You'd better call an ambulance," said Batula. "I just bit my lip."

Count Dracula was sitting in the *White Hearse* pub enjoying a pint of lager when Gilda the Ghost suddenly materialized on the seat next to him. When he'd recovered from his surprise, the plucky Count said: "Good to see you, Gilda. Let me buy you a drink."

"That'd be lovely," said Gilda. "I'll have a gin and tonic."

But when the publican came over, he said: "Sorry, Count, I can't do it."

"But why?"

"We don't serve spirits here."

After Gilda had dematerialized and gone elsewhere for a drink, Count Dracula was finishing his beer when the publican's strong but stupid son suddenly slipped and dropped a full beer keg right on to the Count's glossy black head.

"My goodness! I am sorry," stammered the publican, helping Dracula to his feet. "I hope you're not injured."

"It's all right, my good man," said the Count, brushing off his black cape. "No harm done — it was only light ale."

Gus the Council Gravedigger decided to stop work early one afternoon and go to the cinema. He bought a ticket and went in, but within a minute he was back at the box office buying another. He went in again, but was soon out asking to buy another ticket. After this had gone on a few more times, the ticket seller demanded: "See here, tall dark and grubby, what are you playing at? That's the sixth ticket you've bought in the last fifteen minutes."

"I know," said Gus, "but every time I give my ticket to that old lady in there she tears it up."

In an effort to smarten up her crypt, Gilda the Ghost bought a big carpet that Wanda the Witch had advertised for sale. Huffing and puffing, she carried the big rolled-up carpet home, but Wanda hadn't even finished counting her money before Gilda was back, her usually pale face pink with anger.

"This carpet is no good," she insisted. "I want my money back."

"Why, Gilda," said the witch smoothly, putting the money in her purse, "what's the matter?"

"*This* is the matter," Gilda said, flipping open the carpet to reveal a gaping hole in the middle of it.

"What did you expect?" Wanda the Witch asked. "I *told* you it was in mint condition."

Count and Lady Dracula left Drogo and Creepella with Gilda and took a drive in their Bloodmobile to the seaside. As they stood on a cliff looking down on the waves, Lady Dracula said: “You know, darling, you remind me of the sea.”

“Really, sweetheart?” asked the Count. “Is it because I’m wild, restless and romantic?”

“No, it’s because you make me sick!”

Sam the Skeleton was around at Gilda's crypt playing a game of chess, and Grimly was home from college, so there were lots of people coming and going.

"I wonder, Gilda," said Sam, taking a pawn, "why every time the bell rings your dog, Ghostly, goes into the corner."

"That's simple," replied Gilda, taking Sam's queen. "When he was alive he was a boxer."

The next week Ghostly went missing, and Gilda was very worried about him.

"Why don't you put an advertisement in the *Spirit Times?*" Wanda the Witch asked.

"Don't be dim!" Gilda snapped. "You know Ghostly can't read."

Wanda the Witch was very proud when Rasputin, her black cat, joined the St John Ambulance Brigade.

"He certainly looks smart in his uniform," said Lady Dracula, "but what on earth is he going to do for them?"

"He's going to be a first-aid kitten, naturally," Wanda said.

"Ooh!" said Sam the Skeleton to Wanda the Witch, "I don't see how you can stand to have that Rasputin around. It would make my flesh creep, if I had any. Black cats are unlucky, you know."

"Nonsense," said Wanda.

"No, really," Sam insisted. "I had a friend who was followed by a black cat, and it brought him *very* bad luck."

"What friend was that?"

"Mortimer Mouse."

"I don't know why you bother buying a newspaper," Mr Jolly said to Gus the Council Gravedigger. "Television provides the news a lot faster."

"I still find it pretty useful," said Gus. "Did you ever try to swat a fly with a television set?"

Count Dracula was playing poker with Gus the Council Gravedigger, Sam the Skeleton and Mr Jolly, and he was losing heavily.

"You know," he said, looking around suspiciously, "this game reminds me of poker sessions we used to have when I lived out in Africa."

"How's that?" asked Sam, raking in his winnings.

"There were lots of cheetahs there, too."

Where does Mr Jolly the undertaker get his company's vehicle repaired?
The hearsepital.

Count Dracula was telling the gang down at the *White Hearse* about his latest feat of courage. ". . . without the least concern for my personal safety," he said, "I tackled a burglar in my pyjamas and . . . "

Just then someone interrupted from the back. "How on earth did a burglar get into your pyjamas?"

Creepella Dracula answered the door to an encyclopedia salesman.

"Are your parents in, little girl?" he asked.

"They was in," Creepella said. "But they is out now."

"Tsk, tsk!" said the book salesman. "Where's your grammar?"

"In the front room watching television."

"Mum," asked Grimly Ghost, "would you punish me for something I haven't done?"

"Of course not," said Gilda.

"That's a relief," said Grimly. "I haven't done any haunting homework so far this year, and I've been kicked out of college."

Wanda the Witch was in town one day and saw the most beautiful purple dress in the window of *Ghastly Gowns*. She rushed into the shop, saying: "I must try on that beeeeeee-utiful dress in the window!"

The shop assistant looked at her sniffily and said: "It's not your colour, I don't think it will suit you — and besides, you'll have to use the changing rooms just like everyone else."

Count Dracula got the idea that he was a singer. Every night his awful voice would waft over the cemetery, annoying the dead, irritating the living and grating on the eardrums of every creature in between. Finally, all of the creatures gathered up torches and a stout rope and marched in a body on the Draculas' spooky house. Sam the Skeleton nearly broke his knucklebones on the door, and finally Dracula opened it.

"What do you want? You're disturbing my practice."

Wanda the Witch said: "Count, your voice is worse than torture, and if you don't cut the canary act we're going to hang you and burn down your house. And if that doesn't work, we're going to get tough."

For a moment, Count Dracula was silent. Then he spoke with quiet dignity: "My friends, I get your message. You are not crazy about my vocal efforts. I accept your criticism, and will do as you say if you will grant me one wish only. I wish to sing just one more song, and then I will fall forever silent. Do you agree?"

Everybody cheered and shouted their agreement, but finally they were silent. Then Count Dracula opened his mouth and they heard his beginning words: "Ten million green bottles . . . "

Arnold and his friend were out in the back garden playing ghosts when his mother called out: "Arnold! What are you doing out there?"

"Just doing what comes supernaturally, Mother!" he replied.

Tom and Bill were discussing Gilda's forthcoming Hallowe'en party:
BILL: "I was going to go as a werewolf, but I'm not so sure noooowwwwwwwwwwwwwwwwww!"

Herbert was just about to go out trick-or-treating when his mother asked him: "What are you supposed to be?"

"I'm a wolfman, Mum," he said proudly.

"It looks to me," his mother said, "like you're going to the dogs."

Customer in the café across the street from our cemetery: "Fix me a werewolf sandwich and make it snappy!"

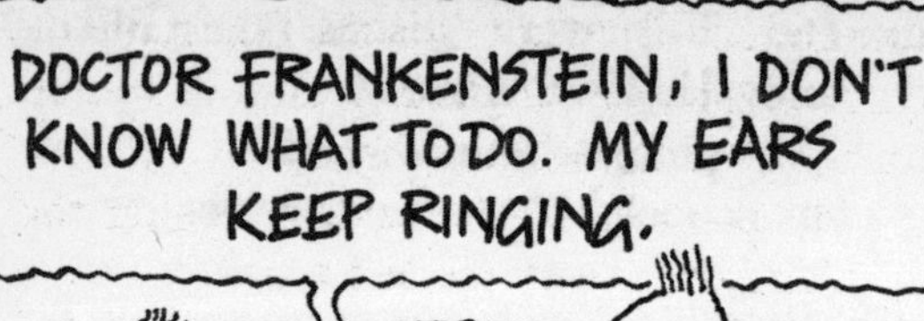

"Go away, Igor," said Dr Frankenstein. "I'm going to be up all night melting glass in this cauldron to make a ten-foot monocle for a giant monster I just created."

"All right," said his assistant, "but don't fall in and make a spectacle of yourself."

Count Dracula invited Gilda the Ghost out on his yacht, *Fangs for the Memory*, and she started to turn green almost immediately.

"My goodness!" she said, clutching the mast. "The sea is very restless today."

"You'd be restless too," Dracula said, "if you had crabs all over your bottom."

When Dr Frankenstein got tired of making monsters, he decided to invent a new automobile fuel which would take the place of petrol. Finally, he shouted: "Igor! Igor! I've done it. I've invented a brand new fuel."

"What is it?" asked Igor.

"This!" said the mad scientist triumphantly, holding up a rabbit by its ears. "When I put this common bunny rabbit into the tank of my car, it will run."

"Possibly," said Igor, "but it will be good only for short hops."

"You're always complaining," Dr Frankenstein told his monster. "What do you want?"

"I'm lonely," said the monster. "Can't you make me a brother?"

"I'm a bit short of spare parts right now," said the mad scientist. "Will you settle for a transistor?"

Dr Frankenstein was in our local pub, *The White Hearse,* drowning his sorrows when Count Dracula sat down next to him. "What's the matter?" asked the Count.

"It's that new monster of mine," said Dr F. "I got the electric wires crossed, and all he does is answer me back."

"Igor," Dr Frankenstein said, "I'm going to pull the switch and bring this monster to life."

"But, Doctor," Igor protested, "you haven't put a brain in yet."

"I couldn't find one. I'm going to do it anyway."

"But, Boss," Igor asked, "how long can a creature live without a brain?"

"I don't know, Igor," the doctor replied. "How old are you, anyway?"

One night, Count Dracula was sound asleep when Lady D shook him awake: "Quick! Quick!" she said. "What does it mean when the barometer falls?"

"Usually that the nail holding it has fallen out of the wall."

"Our little Drogo has a Norwegian penfriend," Lady Dracula told Wanda the Witch. "The only problem is that he doesn't know English."

"But how do they communicate?" asked Wanda.

"Norse code."

Our community policeman found Count Dracula walking around the cemetery at midnight scattering powder from a bag around the tombstones.

"Excuse me, sir," said the bobby, "but what are you doing?"

"I'm scattering anti-zombie powder," said Count D.

"But there are no zombies here," said the policeman.

"Yes, doesn't it work well?" said the Count.

Drogo Dracula was annoying Wanda the Witch at Gilda's party so she turned him into a little woolly lamb.

"What have you done to my little boy?" demanded Countess D. "Speak to me, my boy," she said, kneeling by the side of the lamb. "How do you feel?"

"Very b-a-a-a-a-d!" said Drogo.

Cemetery
Mort
Itian
Champion
the
Wonder
Hearse
Paul
Bearer
Sam
Spade
Silas
Mourner
Orphan
Annie
Bea
Reaved

celebrities
Cass Kett
Artie Ficial-Grass
Mum Morial
M. Baum
Tom B Stone
Effie Taff
Dee Ceased
Morry Bund

Tombstone Rib-Ticklers

Gus the Council gravedigger managed to offend Wanda the Witch, and she put a curse on him. Everything he did went wrong. The ground in the cemetery suddenly seemed as hard as cement, and when he finally managed to dig a grave, it flooded with water; his favourite spade went missing; the cemetery gates rusted closed so that a funeral cortège couldn't get to it. Nothing Gus could do went right until one day he dropped a piece of buttered bread and it landed butterside up.

Racing over to Wanda's mausoleum, Gus told her what had happened. "Does this mean that you've forgiven me?" he asked.

"No," said Wanda spitefully, "I haven't. You just buttered the wrong side of the bread, that's all."

The entire population of the cemetery was a-buzz when they heard that the ghost of a policeman was moving into a Victorian mausoleum near the chapel of rest.

Only Gilda was a bit sniffy about her new neighbour. "I suppose it will be all right if he's one of the higher ranks," she said. "Is he a chief superintendent?"

"No," said Count Dracula. "An inspectre."

Count Dracula claims that Gus the Council gravedigger is so stupid that he thinks that if you ring Interpol they'll send your girlfriend a dozen roses.

Wanda the Witch was sitting in the light of the full moon with her new boyfriend when he said: "I love you, Wanda."

"Of course, you do," Wanda said, "but will you love me when I am old, wrinkled and ugly?"

"What do you mean *when*?"

"I don't know what's wrong with men these days," Wanda the Witch told Gilda. "Just this week I've proposed to five men without avail."

"Try wearing a veil next time!" said Grimly, running through a wall to escape.

Count Dracula was trying to convince Grimly Ghost to marry the count's daughter, Creepella.

"But she's ugly," Grimly objected.

"Not in the dark," said Dracula.

"You haven't given her any dowry."

"That'll prove you're marrying her for love."

"She's so stupid that she thinks an optimist is someone who fits people with spectacles."

"A clever girl would only make you unhappy."

"And worst of all, she's a vampire."

"Nobody's perfect," said Count Dracula.

Dr Frankenstein, who fancied himself as a bit of a match-maker, heard about Count Dracula's search for a husband for Creepella and went to see him. "I've got just the husband for Creepella. You'll have to pay me a little something, but he's young, handsome, rich, a Cambridge graduate, had a brief career in the Royal Marines and is now in show business."

"He sounds promising," said Dracula. "Is he by any chance a vampire?"

"No," admitted Dr F, "but to get a girl like your Creepella, I'm sure he'd consider the possibility."

"Even better," said the Count. "Who is he?"

"Prince Edward."

"*That* Prince Edward?"

"The very same."

Dracula thought for a moment then he said: "All right. It's a deal."

"Terrific," said Dr Frankenstein. "A good decision." He patted his pockets. "Now, where did I put the Queen's phone number?"

Count Dracula couldn't sleep. All night he walked the floor of his bedroom high up in Castle Dracula worrying and worrying. Finally, the creaking floorboards woke Lady D.

"What's the matter with you?" she asked sleepily.

"I can't sleep," said the Count. "I owe Gus the Council gravedigger fifty pounds. It's due tomorrow morning and I haven't got it. What shall I do?"

"Go to sleep," said Lady Dracula. "It's Gus who should be walking the floor with worry."

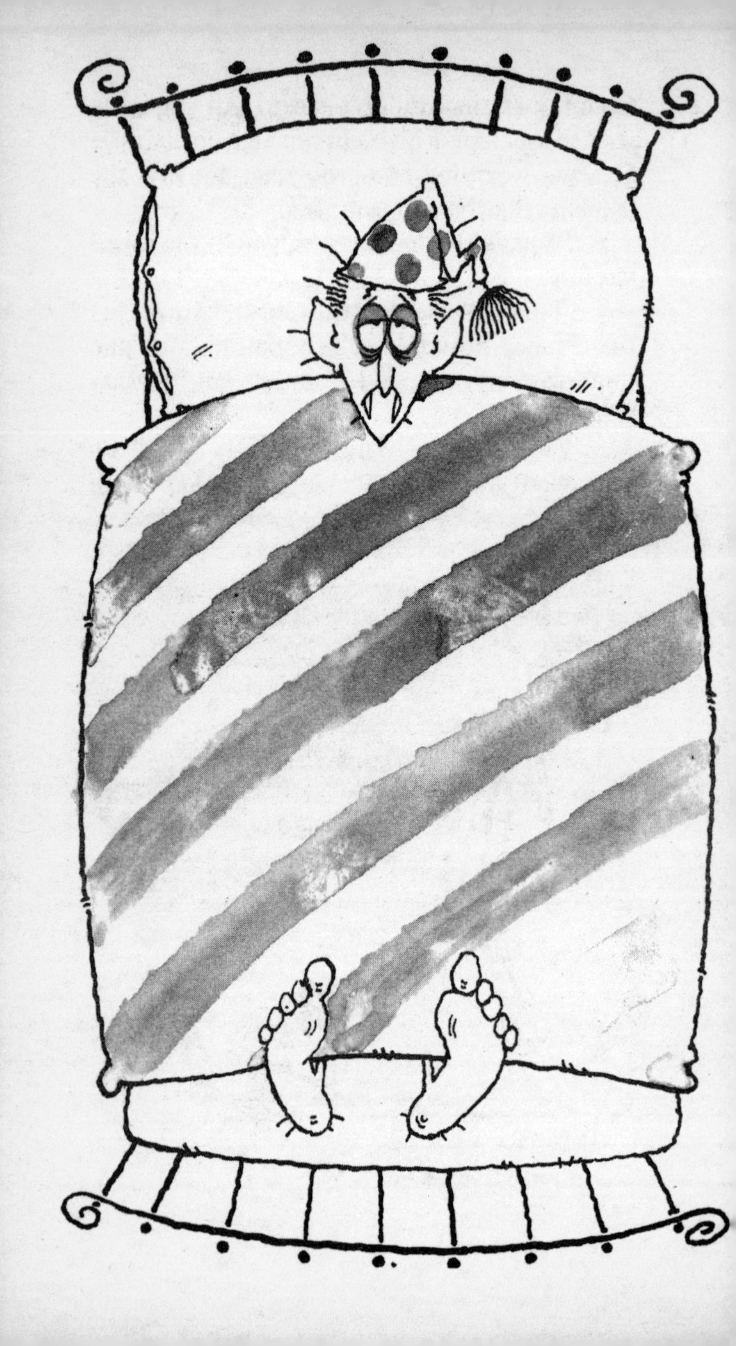

Wanda the Witch was angry with Count Dracula and put a curse on him. At first nothing happened, but then Sam the Skeleton told her that the Count was sick in bed.

Rushing to Dracula's tall, gothic house, Wanda banged on the door. When Lady Dracula opened it, Wanda asked to see the Count.

"I'm sorry," said Lady D, "you can't. The Count has the most terrible boils and he's in agony."

"Oh," said Wanda, and went away.

But five minutes later she was back knocking on the big door.

"I told you," said Lady Dracula, "my husband is sick in bed with boils and can't see anyone."

"Oh," said Wanda, and went away again.

But *three* minutes later she was back knocking louder than ever.

"This is the third time I've told you that the Count has terrible boils and can't see you. Why do you keep pestering me this way?"

"I'm sorry," said Wanda, "but I just can't hear the good news too often!"

When it became necessary to replace the floor of the chapel of rest, Gus the Council gravedigger said he thought the new floor should be sanded and stained.

"No," said Count Dracula, who had an opinion about everything. "Sanded and stained floors are too slippery. The pallbearers will slip and break their necks."

"Rubbish!" said Gus, and for days the two argued. Finally, they called in Mr Jolly the undertaker to settle the argument.

"Well," said Mr Jolly, "there's a lot in what both of you say. Why don't we compromise? We'll sand and stain the boards, but then lay them upside down."

"Did you ever notice," said Gus the Council gravedigger, "that Wanda looks like Helen Green?"

"Yes," said Sam the Skeleton, "and she looks even worse in red."

Wanda went to the new photographer in town and had her photograph taken, but she wasn't very pleased with the results. "To be quite frank," she said, "I don't think these photographs do me justice."

"You don't want justice," said the photographer. "You want mercy."

"Have you heard?" Count Dracula asked Dr Frankenstein. "All the ghosts in the cemetery have gone on strike."

"What are they demanding?"

"A living wage."

"Rasputin," Wanda the Witch demanded of her black cat, "why are you continually scratching yourself behind the ear?"

"Because," said Rasputin, still scratching, "nobody else knows exactly where I itch."

The Honourable Drogo Dracula's wedding to the beautiful young girl was so sad that even the cake was in tiers.

I DON'T THINK I'LL GO TO GILDA'S PARTY.
WHY NOT?

I'VE GOT A LITTLE COLD COMING ON. I'VE GOT THE SNIFFLES, AND BESIDES I DON'T HAVE A COSTUME...
YOU DON'T NEED ONE. YOU CAN GO AS THE UPSIDE-DOWN MAN.

Wanda the Witch was admiring an amazingly large and beautiful diamond that Dracula's wife was wearing. "You're so lucky," she said.

"It's the Dracula diamond, one of the most perfect in the world," the Countess said, "but there's a curse that goes with it."

"What's that?"

"Count Dracula."

The Black Witch was standing waiting for a taxi when, just as one stopped, a big fat ghost brushed past her, stepped heavily on her foot and took her taxi.

"Curse you!" cried the Black Witch after the vanishing taxi. "May you run into a train at the first crossroads."

"Stop!" insisted a passing goblin. "That ghost may be a slob, but think of the poor driver's innocent family."

"All right," said the Witch grudgingly, shouting after the taxi: "You shouldn't run into a train at the next crossing."

"And do you know?" the impressed goblin told a crowd of headless spirits. "It didn't."

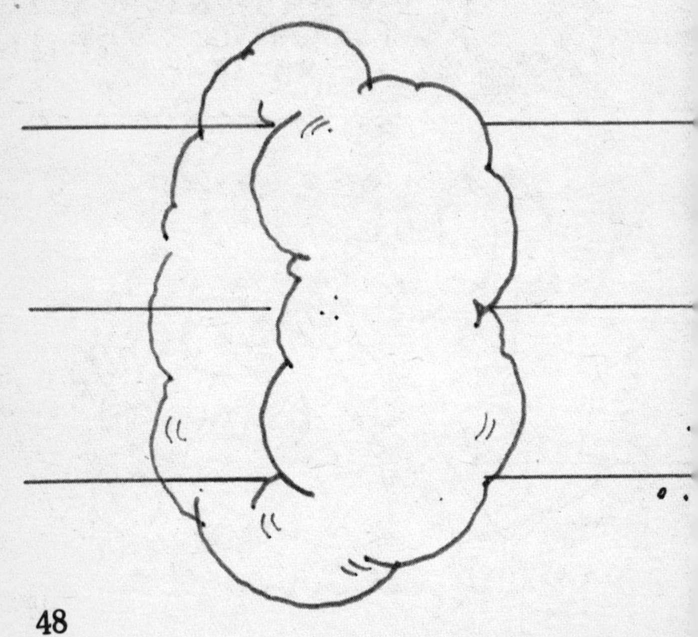

Dracula was wheeling a barrow through the cobbled streets one day when Frankenstein looked into it. "Ugh!" he said. "What are *those*?"

"Pig skins," said Dracula.

"What on earth are you going to do with them?"

"How else do you expect me to hold my pigs together?"

The witch went to see a psychiatrist. "You must help me, doctor," she cried. "My cat thinks he's a five-pound note."

"Don't worry," said the doctor. "Just take him out shopping. The change will do him good."

Dracula laboured hard and long to build a boat in the back garden of his castle, but it was very peculiar looking.

"What do you call that?" asked his uncle.

"A blood vessel," Dracula said proudly.

"Why on earth does Rasputin keep twitching his tail?" the gravedigger asked Wanda the Witch.

"Do you know anyone who would twitch it for him?" she demanded.

Dracula was sitting in front of his fire one night looking through a catalogue of people when he heard a loud banging on his massive front door.

When he opened it, he found the Mad Monk from next door, who demanded: "Do you believe in free speech?"

"Well," said Dracula, "as it happens, I do. Why?"

"I want to use your telephone."

"I'm really worried," Wanda the Witch confided to her favourite broomstick. "I keep seeing polka-dotted vampires."

"Have you seen a psychiatrist?" asked the broomstick.

"No," said Wanda, "just polka-dotted vampires."

Merlin was raving like a madman: "I've simply got to have a cup of tea, I tell you, and all we've got in the house is coffee."

"Is that so bad?" asked his hunchbacked assistant.

"Bad?" demanded Merlin. "Bad? What good is a sorcerer without a cuppa?"

"That's Mozart," said Count Dracula, pointing at a passing figure, "the great decomposer."

"Don't you mean *composer*?" asked the Mad Friar.

"Not since *I've* known him," said Dracula.

"You've gone back to wearing that black, pointed hat," the poisoned toad remarked to the witch. "I thought you'd switched to a porkpie model."

"I did," said the witch, "but I had to give it up. The gravy kept running down my neck."

"Here!" complained the Hermit to the Lord of Baskerville Manor. "Your hound has bitten me on the leg."

"Oh, dear!" said his Lordship. "Did you put anything on it?"

"No. He seemed to like it just the way it was."

"I'm afraid that Wanda the Witch has put a spell on me," said the dwarf, beginning to turn purple with green bumps.

"Just turn around, face that window and stick your tongue out as far as you can," advised Marie Antoinette.

"Will that help?"

"Probably not," said the headless queen, "but that nasty Napoleon Bonaparte is passing, and I hate him."

"I'm a bit worried about this adder bite," said Dracula. "My leg is beginning to swell and I soon won't be able to get my trousers on."

"Don't worry," said King MacBeth, "I'll lend you a kilt."

Gilda was sitting in the middle row at the cinema, and as she got up to buy some sweets, she stepped heavily on Count Dracula's foot. When she returned with a bag full of bat's knuckles she stopped next to Count Dracula's seat at the end of the row and asked: "Count, did I step on your foot just now?"

"Yes, you did," the Count said, expecting an apology.

"Oh, good!" Wanda said. "This must be my row then."

One day Wanda was flying on her broom over the Dark Forest when she spotted Petulia the Poisoner drowning in a mossy pool. With a gesture of her hand, she dried up the pond and saved Petulia's life.

"That was very good of you," Gilda the Ghost told her. "Why are you looking so worried?"

"It's just," said Wanda, "that Petulia's so grateful that she's promised to bake me a cake."

"Help! Help!" cried Gus the Council Gravedigger. "I was digging that grave over there, and a phantom flew out and bit me."

"That's terrible!" said Mrs Gus. "You'll be dead in four minutes."

"Can't you do anything for me?" he begged.

"I could boil you an egg," suggested his wife.

"I'm feeling much better today," Wanda the Witch told her doctor.

"That's good," the doctor said. "You can get up for a spell this afternoon."

Our local policeman arrested Count Dracula and charged him with killing time.

"Not guilty," said the Count. "The clock struck first."

Our cemetery is the only one in the country with a beach, and luckily we have a ghost guard.

Count Dracula was angry with Gilda the Ghost's cousin Rudy and challenged him to a boxing match.

"Don't worry," Gilda told Rudy. "As a boxer, Dracula is just like a candle."

"How do you mean?"

"One good blow will put him out."

The Red Witch was absolutely terrible at putting spells on people but then one day she turned Gus the Council Gravedigger into a fire hydrant.

"That's wonderful!" admired Gilda. "But how have you suddenly got such powers?"

"Oh," said the Red Witch, "I had a tranceplant."

Count Dracula walked up to a perfect stanger passing our cemetery and said: "I'll bet you £10 I can tell you what you do for a living."

"Nonsense!" said the stranger, whipping out his wallet.

"Well," said the Count, "you're an undertaker. Am I right?"

"How did you guess?" the undertaker said, paying up.

"Easy," said the Count. "It was your grave manner."

HONESTLY, DROGO, YOUR TABLE MANNERS ARE ATROCIOUS! HAVEN'T YOU GOT A TONGUE?
CERTAINLY, MATER, BUT MY ARMS ARE LONGER!

One evening at the supper table, Count Dracula said: "Drogo, I don't believe they're putting anything in your thick head at that expensive school I send you to. For instance, give me a sentence using the word 'indisposition'."

"That's easy, old sport," said Drogo. "I'm sitting in this chair because it's easier to reach the food indisposition."

Wanda the Witch and Rasputin were watching television one evening when a football game came on. "I'ate football players," said Rasputin, hitting the remote control button to switch over.

"Really?" asked Wanda. "What did they taste like?"

"Mum! Mum!" cried Grimly, "there's a vampire bat in my soup."

"What did you expect?" asked Gilda the Ghost. "It's blood soup, isn't it?"

To make up for the tricks she'd played on him, Wanda the Witch invited Gus the Council Gravedigger in for a bit of lunch and served him a steaming bowl of soup.

"What is this?" Gus asked, after taking a sip.

"It's bean soup," said Wanda.

"Quite possibly," Gus said, spitting it out. "But what's it *now*?"

"Mum," asked Drogo one day after school, "What's slimy and has eyeballs in it?"

"I don't know," said Lady S, "but it sounds delicious."

"School tapioca," said Drogo.

"Ugh!"

"Poor Wanda's in the hospital suffering from shock," Gus the Council Gravedigger told Sam the Skeleton.

"Why? What happened?"

"She stepped on a bun and a currant ran up her leg."

The local bobby came knocking on the door of Count Dracula's house the other evening to enquire about a young woman who'd been badly frightened when a tall, pale-faced man wearing a black cape leapt out from behind a bush at her.

"It couldn't have been me, officer," said the Count. "I haven't attacked anyone since 1845."

"Are you sure?" demanded the policeman.

"Cross my heart," said the Count, shuddering at the image.

"All right," said the policeman, "but I'll be watching you."

"Who was that, dear?" Countess D called.

"No one important," replied Dracula. "We'd better hurry if we're going to catch that film. It begins at 1915."

Gus the Council Gravedigger was having a terrible time getting the tombstone straight on a grave he'd just dug.

"Darn it!" he said, backing off and nearly falling into another new grave. "I just can't get it right."

"Here," said Gilda the Ghost helpfully. "Try this spirit level."

Mr Jolly the undertaker and a crowd of mourners stood impatiently by the side of a freshly-dug grave, but there was no sign of the hearse carrying the deceased.

Finally, twenty minutes late, the hearse drove into our cemetery and the driver jumped out. "What on earth kept you?" demanded Mr Jolly.

"Well," explained the driver, "I was obeying the sign out on the street there, it says DRIVE SLOWLY: CEMETERY ENTRANCE AHEAD.

Last Christmas, the Honourable Drogo was very disappointed by his present from the Count.

"You *are* ungrateful," said Lady D. "That's a lovely pocket calculator your father gave you."

"Sure, mater," said Drogo, "but I already *know* how many pockets I've got."

Our vicar ran screaming into the doctor's office, crying: "Help! Help! I've been bitten by a vampire bat!"

"Not to worry," said the nurse, "I'll put some cream on it."

"Don't be silly," said the vicar. "It'll be miles away by now."

The stonemason from Mr Jolly's undertaking establishment was carving the name on a tombstone when he stopped and scratched his head. "I can't make out how to spell this name," he said. "Is it *Llewellyn* or *Llewelyn*?"

"I'm not sure," said Gus the Council Gravedigger, peering at the piece of paper. "And I can't see that it makes all that much difference."

"You don't, eh?" said the stonemason. "Well, it will make one L of a difference to his family!"

"Did you hear", Gilda the Ghost asked Wanda the Witch, "that Count Dracula has a brand new car?"

"Do tell!" said Wanda. "What type is it?"

"A Rolls Canardly."

"A Rolls Canardly? What sort of a car is that?"

"Well," said Gilda, "it's a car that rolls down one hill and canardly get up the next."

One day, the Honourable Drogo came home from school with a medal pinned on his smart uniform.

"What's that for?" Countess Dracula asked.

"I saved the entire school," said Drogo.

"What a peculiar thing to do!" said his mother. "But how exactly did you do that?"

"I bit the school cook."

Gilda Ghost's Shopping List

surgical spirits
witch hazel
skeleton key
ghoulash
blood vessels
ghost towels
sirlion stake

Creepy Questions

Why does the Headless Nun wear black?
It's just a little habit she got into.

How does a spirit in California communicate with a spirit in New York?
Ghost to ghost.

Why is Count Dracula poor?
Because he's always getting into the red.

Did you hear about the clergyman who got fired for burying the wrong body in the wrong hole?
It was a grave mistake.

What haunts Blackpool and Brighton?
A sandwitch.

What are dangerous and sit in a glass of water in the bathroom?
Count Dracula's teeth.

What's the difference between a Seville orange and Dr Frankenstein's latest monstrous creation?
The orange has only one navel.

When he took up watercolouring as a hobby, why would Count Dracula never paint the butcher's window?
He was afraid of getting a steak in his art.

Why does Dr Frankenstein call his girlfriend "treasure"?
Because he dug her up.

What did Grimly Ghost say to Sam the Skeleton?
I've got a bone to pick with you.

Why did Baldy Banshee paint rabbits on his skull?
Because he hoped that they would look like hares from a distance.

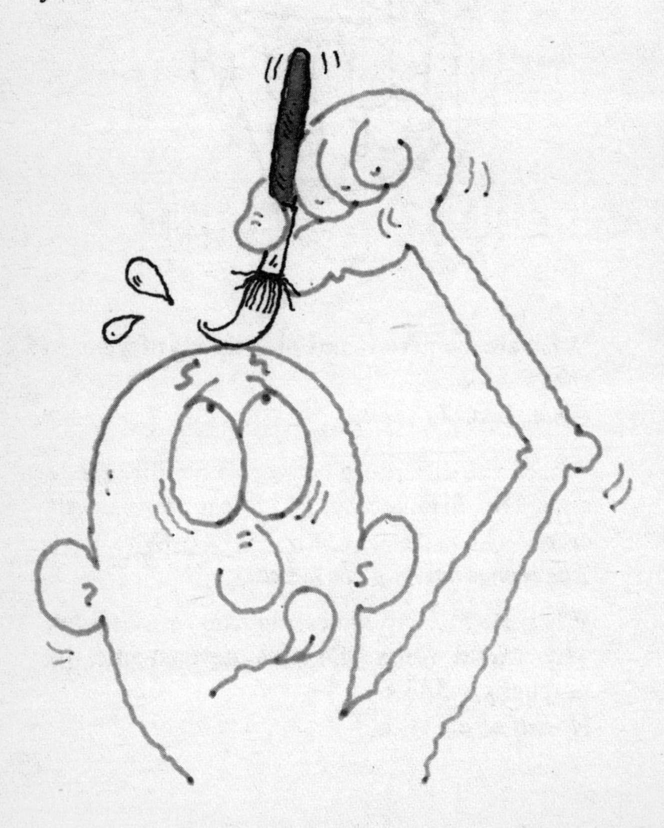

Why was the skeleton a coward?
Because he had no guts.

Why did Dracula steal a seahorse?
So he could play water polo.

Why do vampires brush their teeth twice a day?
To keep from having bat breath.

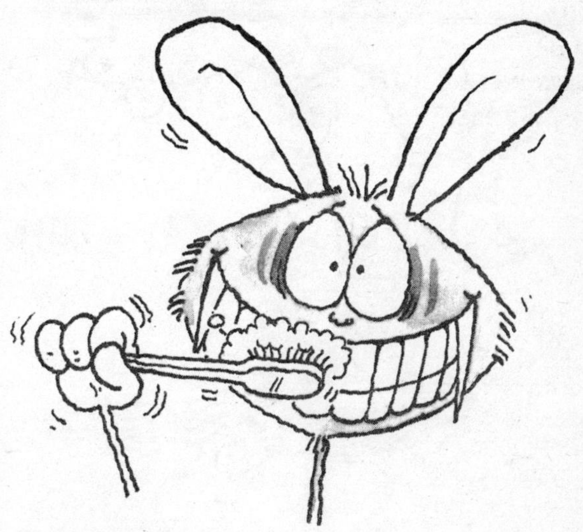

Where do spirits stay when they go to the seaside?
At ghost houses.

When Count Dracula went to Germany, what was his favourite snack?
A Frankfurter.

If you went to the Skeleton's Ball, what would you have?
A rattling good time.

What kind of fur do you get from a werewolf?
As fur as you can.

Why is Count Dracula a good house guest?
Because he eats necks to nothing.

What fruit does Count Dracula like best of all?
Nectarines.

Why didn't Dr Frankenstein mind when everybody turned against him?
Because he can always make new friends.

What is Wanda the Witch's favourite part of the newspaper?
The horror-scope.

What is Count Dracula's favourite soup?
Scream of tomato.

What is Count Dracula's favourite cocktail?
A Bloody Mary.

What do you get when you cross a ghost with a packet of crisps?
Snacks that go bump in the night.

What disturbed Gus the Council gravedigger's nap in the Chapel of Rest?
All the coffin there.

Why did the witch's brother go to the hospital?
To have his ghoulstones removed.

When the gang from the cemetery play football, who defends against penalties?
The ghoulie, of course.

Who did the vampire want to marry?
The girl necks door.

Why did Count Dracula refuse to move to Scunthorpe?
Because he'd heard it was a one-hearse town.

"Drink up your milk, darling," said the mother skeleton. "It's very good for your bones."

Why did Count Dracula have an appointment with the manager of the blood bank?
He wanted to apply for an overdraught.

What would you need if you accidentally got locked in our cemetery after hours?
A skeleton key.

What do spooks wear while driving a car?
Sheetbelts.

What's the difference between
Dr Frankenstein and an elephant?
An elephant remembers while Dr F dismembers.

What is yellow and white and flies at
200 miles an hour?
Wanda the Witch's egg sandwich.

What has fangs, wears a black cape and is over ten feet tall?
Count Dracula on stilts.

What did Dr Frankenstein say to the corpse as he put it back in its grave?
That's about enough out of you.

What do you call the Red Witch's new two-wheeled motorized vehicle?
A brrrrrrroooooooomstick.

Why did Herman the Ghost sit in the corner at the disco?
Because he had no body to dance with.

What did they call the Invisible Man after his wife had a baby?
Transparent.

How does the vicar know when to start his sermon at a funeral?
He waits until the coughin' stops.

Why did Dr Frankenstein decide to build his latest monster in church?
He said he wanted to perform an organ transplant.

What would you get if a rooster decided to fight a hundred ghosts?
Creamed chicken.

Where does Frankenstein's monster sleep?
Anywhere he chooses!

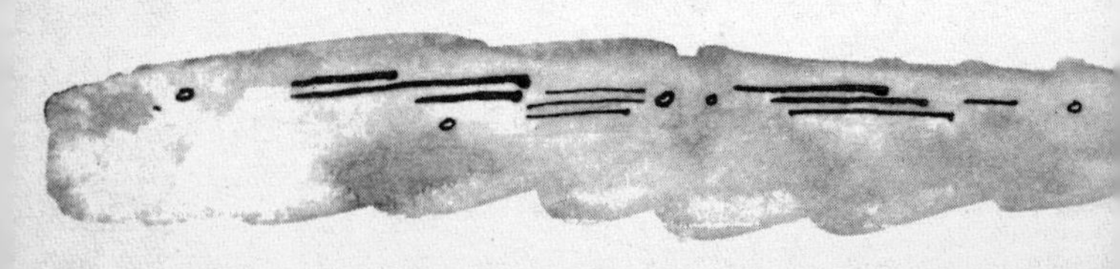

Best sellers of

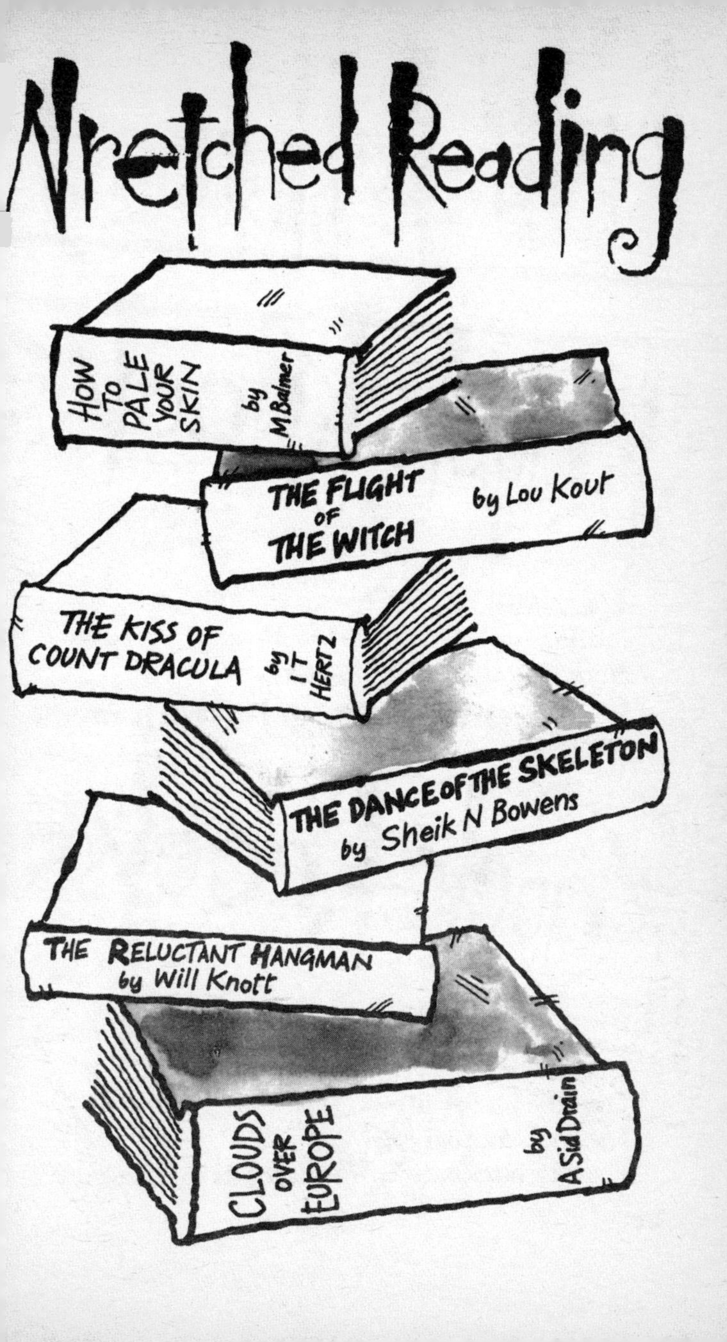
Wretched Reading
HOW TO PALE YOUR SKIN
by M.Balmer
THE FLIGHT OF THE WITCH
by Lou Kout
THE KISS OF COUNT DRACULA
by I T HERTZ
THE DANCE OF THE SKELETON
by Sheik N Bowens
THE RELUCTANT HANGMAN
by Will Knott
CLOUDS OVER EUROPE
by A Sid Drain

Nail-Biting

Knock-Knock

Who's there?
Coffin.
Hack! Hack! Sorry, Coffin who?
Coffin my face once more, and I'll punch you in the nose!

Who's there?
The little black bat.
The little black bat who?
The little black bat who's going to bite your neck!

Knock-Knocks

Knock-Knock

Who's there?
Witches.
Witches who?
Witch's the way to go home?

Knock-Knock

Who's there?
Boo!
Boo who?
Don't cry. I didn't mean it.

The Hunchback of Notre Dame and a similarly afflicted friend were walking home from the pub one night when they came to our cemetery.

"Oh, no!" said the Hunchback of Notre Dame. "I'm not walking through there. It's haunted."

"But it's a much shorter way," said his friend.

"You go ahead, and I'll meet you on the other side," said the Hunchback of Notre Dame.

So his friend walked into the cemetery, and he hadn't gone more than a hundred yards when a ghost suddenly sprang up in front of him and demanded: "What's that on your back, then?"

"It's — it's a h-hump!" came the worried response.

"Well, then," said the ghost, "I'll have that," and he reached out and snatched the hump off his back.

Suddenly, the hunchback could stand up straight for the first time in years. He was enjoying the sensation when he walked out of the cemetery and met the Hunchback of Notre Dame, who demanded: "What happened to you?" His friend told him, so the Hunchback of Notre Dame went rushing into the cemetery until he too met the ghost, who demanded: "What's that on your back, then?"

"A hump," he was told.

"Well, then," said the ghost, reaching out his hand, "have another one."

"Pssst!" said a voice from behind the big mausoleum. "Do you want to see a man eating cod?"

"Well, yes, that would interesting."

"Go down to the fish and chip shop, then."

When Wanda the Witch and Gilda the Ghost get a bit tipsy, they like to go for a tramp in the cemetery.

Fortunately, they're usually too drunk to catch him.

On a bleak and moonless night, Gus the Council gravedigger returned to the cemetery to get the lunchbox he'd forgotten, when he saw an old man chipping away at a tombstone with a hammer and chisel.

"Here!" Gus demanded. "What do you think you're doing?"

"They spelled my name wrong," grumbled the old man.

Count Dracula and Wanda the Witch got into an argument which soon turned into an exchange of insults. "You", said the Count, "are the sort of witch *Which*? Magazine declares to be a 'worst buy'."

"And you", retorted Wanda, "are the sort of person who gives vampires a bad name!"

Dear Auntie, is it proper to eat fried chicken with the fingers?
No, dear. You should eat the fingers separately.

The Honourable Drogo kept pestering his father with questions: "What is blood made of? What do spirits eat for breakfast? How many ghosts can dance on the point of a pin?" etc., etc., etc., until Count Dracula got fed up with it.

"Don't pester me with so many questions, Drogo!" he said, "What do you think would have happened if I'd asked *my* father so many questions?"

"Well, Pater," Drogo said, "perhaps you'd have been able to answer some of mine."

The lady cannibal arrived at Gilda's Halloween party with a man dressed as a missionary.

"Is that your date?" someone asked.

"No," she said. "My lunch."

The Honourable Drogo Dracula was raving about a girl he'd met at the costume party.

"She's just my type," he claimed.

"And what's that?"

"A positive."

The Honourable Drogo Dracula came home from school with a black eye.

"Oh, Drogo!" said Lady D. "Surely you haven't been fighting? Didn't I tell you that nice boys don't fight?"

"Yes, Mater," said Drogo, "and I thought that the boy sitting next to me was a nice boy until I hit him and found out that he wasn't."

The mummy's little girl wanted to be a Brownie more than anything else in the world, but she was too shy to ask. Finally, she got up the courage to go around to the school hall where the local group met. She returned dancing with joy and told the mummy: "Good news! Brown Owl says that if I go along next week she'll unroll me."

Count Dracula got tired of people from our cemetery sneaking over his twelve-foot wall topped with broken glass and barbed wire to swim in his pool, so he imported some especially vicious alligators.

Despite this, a couple of reckless young ghouls climbed over and were having a swim when suddenly one shouted: "Hey! An alligator has just snapped off my leg."

"Which one?" cried the other ghoul, jumping out of the pool.

"Hard to say," said the first ghoul. "Alligators all look alike to me."

Overheard at a restaurant:

"Hey, you in the space suit! Do you want to see some flying saucers?"

"Yes. How?"

"Just go over there and pinch that waitress."

"Why did you take a punch at that fellow carrying the crystal ball?"

"Well, my psychiatrist says I am too erratic and should try to strike a happy medium."

"I thought you were dressing as a witch again this year?"

"No, I was down in the dumps so I decided to buy a new costume."

"I always wondered where you got them."

Count Dracula took Lady D and little Drogo to the seaside, and they all had a very good time. But when the others were ready to leave, Dracula was still pacing up and down the beach, scraping anxiously through the sand with a stick.

"What are you looking for?" Lady Dracula demanded. "We want to go home."

"I've lost a piece of toffee," Count D said.

"Oh, do come!" his wife insisted. "I'll buy you another piece."

"I've got to find *this* one," the Count insisted. "It's got my fangs stuck to it."

Gus the Council Gravedigger got a little drunk after work one night and found himself up before the magistrate.

"That'll be ten pounds fine, Gus," said the magistrate, "and I hope this will be the last time you appear before me."

"Why's that, judge?" Gus asked. "Are you retiring?"

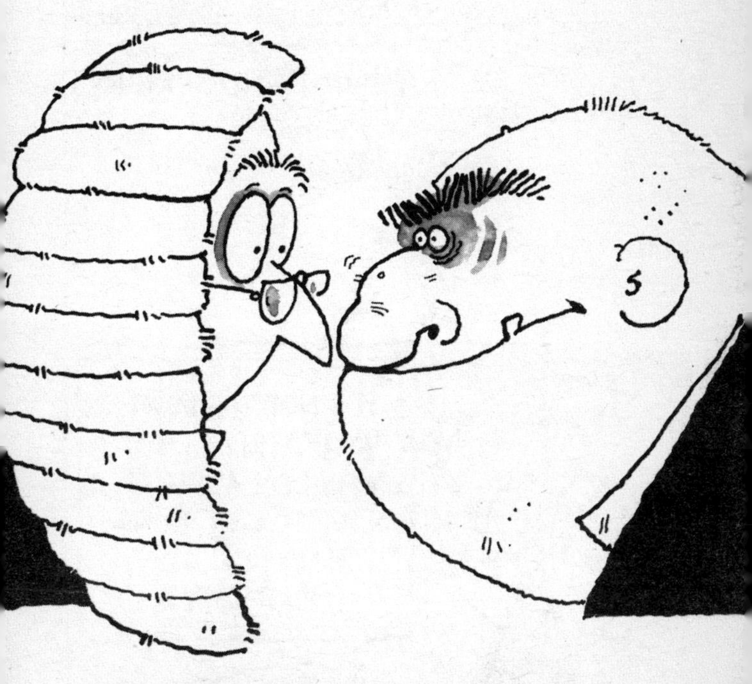

"Have you ever been up before me?" the judge asked Gus.

"I don't know," Gus said. "What time is your alarm clock set for?"

"If you don't behave, I'll clear the courtroom," said the judge angrily when all the gang from the cemetery started laughing at this.

"I thought you had janitors to do that kind of work," said Gus.

"Order! Order!" demanded the magistrate.

"A pint of blood!" called out Count Dracula. "In a straight glass."

Prunella went to Gilda the Ghost's Halloween party but she stood out a mile among the sheets and chains and tatters because she was dressed in a neat blue suit, low-heeled shoes and a smart little hat.

"And just what are *you* supposed to be?" demanded Hermione.

"An air ghostess," said Prunella with a haunting smile.

Did you hear about the two boys who agreed to meet at the Halloween party but missed each other because they both went as the Invisible Man?

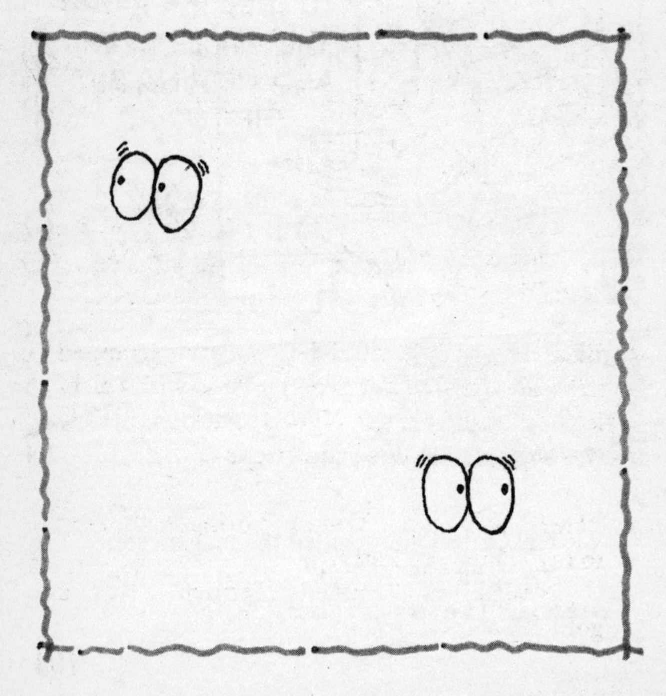

Elsie showed up at the Halloween party wrapped in bread, smeared in mayonnaise and with a bit of lettuce behind her ear. Nobody guessed that she was supposed to be a sandwitch.

"Hey!" said Elsie. "You can't bring that turkey to my Halloween Party."

"Why not?" asked Herman. "It's a goblin."

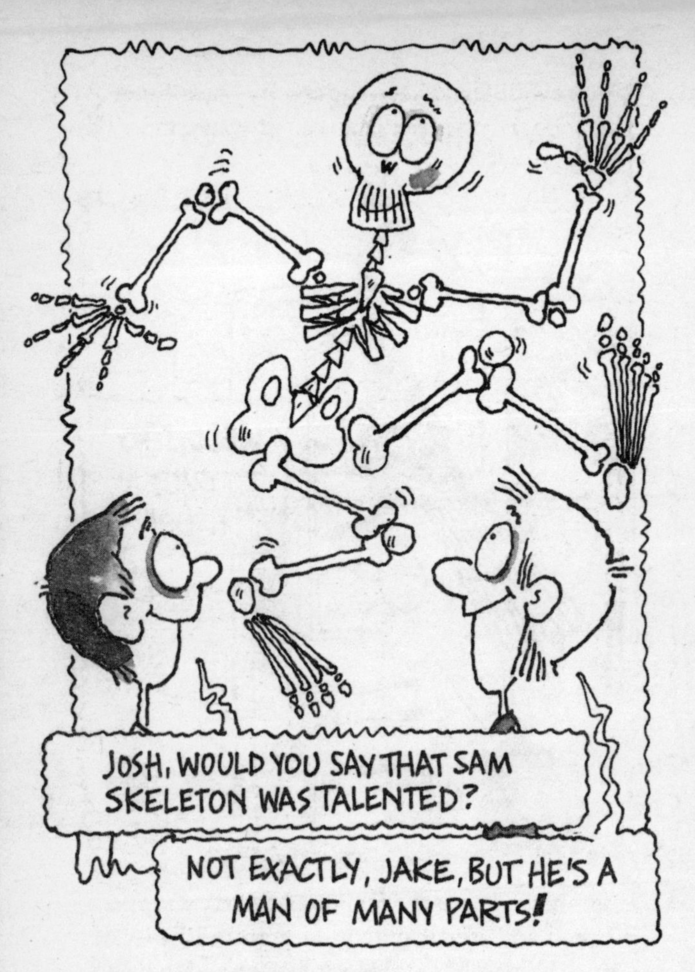

Did you hear about the cemetery keeper who called in a bicycle repairman because some of his spooks were missing?

"Watch out for that vampire bat!" the witch warned the black cat. "He'll put the bite on you."

"You should have seen the creepy ghost I met at the school Halloween party," Cathy said. "It had no nose."

"No nose?" Jane asked. "How did it smell?"

"Terrible!"

"I was worried about you getting home safely," Mary said. "It was so dark outside and you had to go through the cemetery."

"No problem," said Tom. "I was carrying a torch."

"Does that make you safe?"

"It does if you carry it fast enough."

Sam the Skeleton won the prize for best costume and it turned out to be a brand-new comb. "Thanks!" he said, "I'll never part with it."

"The highlight of our Halloween party was a beauty contest."

"Who won?"

"No body."

"It was terrible," Jane said. "I went as Anne Boleyn, and in the crush I lost my head."

"What did you do?"

"I sent for a headhunter, of course."

Nobody could work out what Jimmy's costume was supposed to be. It was big and round and purple, and he kept running round in circles.

"All right!" they said. "We give up. What is it?"

"The Planet of the Grapes!"

George found Ronald walking around on 1st November wearing his costume.

"I've told you a thousand times", George said, "that Halloween is on 31st October."

"I forgot."

"No, you didn't. My words just went in one head and out the other."

Phil was running around trying to put together his Halloween costume. Soon he had everything except for a black belt, and he couldn't find one anywhere. "I've simply got to have a black belt," he told his friend Andy, "or I won't be able to go as Dracula."

"But why", asked Andy, "do you have to have a *black* belt?"

"To keep my trousers up."

When they announced the competition for the best ghost costume, Henry went up on stage wearing his ordinary school clothes but carrying two huge clocks.

"What sort of ghost are you supposed to be?" asked the judge.

"The spirit of the times."

WHAT DO YOU THINK OF MY COSTUME?
IT'S OKAY IF YOU'RE SUPPOSED TO BE AND UNMADE BED!
I'M MAKING A TERRIFIC MASK WITH A NOSE TWELVE INCHES LONG!
YOU CAN'T DO THAT. IF IT WAS TWELVE INCHES IT WOULD BE A FOOT!

ARTHUR: (*throwing back his head and making all sorts of weird noises in his throat*) There! Can you guess what I am?
TOM: I give up.
ARTHUR: A gargoyle!

After they met at a Halloween party, Bob walked Carol home. "I know this is awfully sudden," he said, "but I want you to be my ghoul friend."

While dressing for the party Jerry put on his skeleton costume but couldn't find the head, so he put on an old deerstalker hat instead.

"What are *you* supposed to be?" a friend demanded.

"Sherlock Bones."

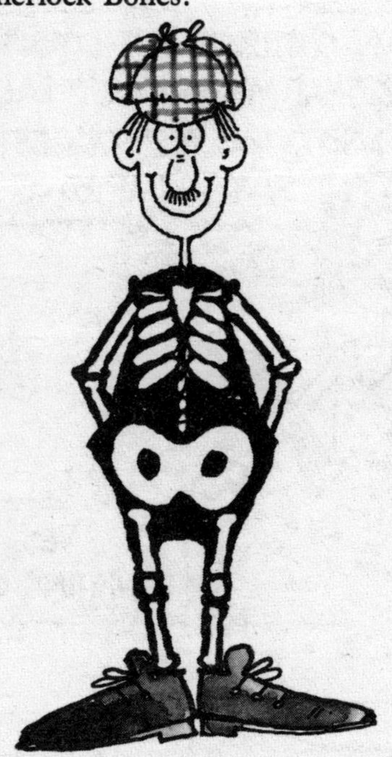

"I give up," said the costume contest judge, looking over the four boys. One was deathly pale and had long flowing hair and the other three carried a coffin. "What are you supposed to be dressed as?"

"Ghouldilocks and the three pall-bearers," was the answer.

HALLOWE'EN Hit Parade

If you were the only ghoul in the world

Yesterdie

Hearse of the Rising Sun

Demons are a ghoul's best friend

Fangs for the Memory

That's the Way it Ghost

Smoke (from the crematorium) gets in your eyes

EERIE EPITAPHS

(Epitaph on a Schoolmaster's Tombstone)

Latin's a dead language
As dead as can be
It killed off all the Romans
And now it's done for me.

Here lies Jeremy Whisson
Crossed a level crossing and didn't look —
Or listen.

(From Boot Hill Cemetery, Tombstone, Arizona)
Here lies the remains of Bill Collins
Drew first — fired last.

JUGGLERS

There are books to suit everyone in Hippo's JUGGLERS series:

When I Lived Down Cuckoo Lane
by Jean Wills £1.75
A small girl and her family move into a new house in Cuckoo Lane. Follow her adventures through the year as she makes friends, starts a new school, learns to ride a bike, and even helps out at her father's shop.

The Secret of Bone Island by Sam McBratney £1.75
Linda, Peter and Gareth are very curious about Bone Island. Especially when they're told some weird stories about the island's history. And then three suspicious-looking men warn them to stay away from the island . . .

Stan's Galactic Bug by John Emlyn Edwards £1.75
Stan can't believe his eyes when his computer game traps an alien from outer space. It's up to Stan to save the intergalactic traveller from destruction!

As If By Magic by Jo Furminger £1.75
Natasha has never seen a girl as weird as Harriet – the new girl in the class. But not only does she *look* strange, with her dark tatty clothes and bright green eyes, but the oddest things start to happen when she's around.

Look out for these other titles in the JUGGLERS series:

Bags of Trouble by Michael Harrison
The Jiggery-Pokery Cup by Angela Bull

MARLENE MARLOWE INVESTIGATES

My name is Marlene. Marlene Marlowe. And I'm the dottiest detective ever to have missed a clue . . .

Follow the hilarious trail of the world's most clueless private eye in these books by Hippo:

Marlene Marlowe Investigates the Great Christmas Pudding Mystery £1.75

Early one morning Marlene is woken by a phonecall: "Come to Peregrine Postlethwaite's bakery immediately!" In the dimly-lit building Marlene follows a trail of dark red sticky mess, leading to a large moving bundle . . .

Marlene Marlowe Investigates the Missing Tapes Affair £1.75

A phonecall summons Marlene to the house of an old friend. There, slumped on the kitchen floor, lies the twisted body of a young man . . .

HAUNTINGS by Hippo Books is a new series of excellent ghost stories for older readers.

Ghost Abbey by Robert Westall
When Maggie and her family move into a run-down old abbey, they begin to notice some very strange things going on in the rambling old building. Is there any truth in the rumour that the abbey is haunted?

Don't Go Near the Water by Carolyn Sloan
Brendan knew instinctively that he shouldn't go near Blackwater Lake. Especially that summer, when the water level was so low. But what was the dark secret that lurked in the depths of the lake?

Voices by Joan Aiken
Julia had been told by people in the village that Harkin House was haunted. And ever since moving in to the house for the summer, she'd been troubled by violent dreams. What had happened in the old house's turbulent past?

The Nightmare Man by Tessa Krailing
Alex first sees the man of his darkest dreams at Stackfield Pond. And soon afterwards he and his family move in to the old house near the pond — End House — and the nightmare man becomes more than just a dream.

A Wish at the Baby's Grave by Angela Bull
Desperate for some money, Cathy makes a wish for some at the baby's grave in the local cemetery. Straight afterwards, she finds a job at an old bakery. But there's something very strange about the bakery and the two Germans who work there. . .

The Bone-Dog by Susan Price
Susan can hardly believe her eyes when her uncle Bryan makes her a pet out of an old fox-fur, a bone and some drops of blood — and then brings it to life. It's wonderful to have a pet which follows her every command — until the bone-dog starts to obey even her unconscious thoughts. . .

All on a Winter's Day by Lisa Taylor
Lucy and Hugh wake up suddenly one wintry morning to find everything's changed — their mother's disappeared, the house is different, and there are two ghostly children and their evil-looking aunt in the house. What has happened?

The Old Man on a Horse by Robert Westall
Tobias couldn't understand what was happening. His parents and little sister had gone to Stonehenge with the hippies, and his father was arrested. Then his mother disappeared. But while sheltering with his sister in a barn, he finds a statue of an old man on a horse, and Tobias and Greta find themselves transported to the time of the Civil War. . .

Look out for these forthcoming titles in the HAUNTING series:
The Rain Ghost by Garry Kilworth
The Haunting of Sophy Bartholomew by Elizabeth Lindsay

SAMANTHA SLADE

Samantha Slade's an ordinary girl living in an ordinary town; but when she starts a job out of school babysitting for the Brown children, her uneventful life is turned upside down. Because when Dr Brown tells Samantha her children are little monsters, poor Sam doesn't realize that they really *are* monsters! Lupi turns into a werewolf when the moon is full, and Drake sprouts fangs, drinks tomato ketchup by the crateful and concocts the most amazing potions in his laboratory!

Book 1: **Monster-Sitter**

When Samantha Slade agrees to let Lupi and Drake Brown, the two children she babysits, help her with the school Halloween party, she finds she's created the most realistic haunted house ever! Lupi turns into a real werewolf, the fake creepie crawlies become alive, and the whole thing turns into a riot of terrified kids . . .

Book 2: **Confessions of a Teenage Frog**

Samantha Slade should have known better than to accept help from Lupi and Drake when she's campaigning to become class president. Drake makes her a "greatness potion", and before she knows it, she's been turned into a frog! Will Drake be able to turn her back again before she has to make her big speech for the campaign?

Book 3: **Our Friend: Public Nuisance No 1**

Sam can hardly believe her eyes when she sees the Browns' new pet – a massive creature that looks like a dinosaur and honks like a goose! And when the monster breaks loose, it's up to Samantha and her babysitting kids to find it before anyone else does . . .

Book 4: **The Terrors of Rock and Roll**

When Samantha hears about the Battle of the Bands competition, she decides to form her own rock group. Then Lupi and Drake, the two kids she babysits, join in with the idea of making a music video. Their "special effects" include hundreds of spiders let loose at the audience, and performing with a live boa constrictor. This time Sam's really scared that things are getting out of control . . .